Don't Write Me Off

Don't Write Me Off

Inspiring Youths to Take the Lead

> Cheryl,
> Just want to say a big "thank you" to you for your kind contributions to our HR Connections class. Your expertise is awe-inspiring. God bless you.
> Ajagu

Anuli Ausbeth-Ajagu   Dec 2013

authorHOUSE®

AuthorHouse™
1663 Liberty Drive
Bloomington, IN 47403
www.authorhouse.com
Phone: 1-800-839-8640

© 2013 by Anuli Ausbeth-Ajagu. All rights reserved.

No part of this book may be reproduced, stored in a retrieval system, or transmitted by any means without the written permission of the author.

Published by AuthorHouse   02/13/2013

ISBN: 978-1-4817-8307-1 (sc)
ISBN: 978-1-4817-8308-8 (e)

Any people depicted in stock imagery provided by Thinkstock are models, and such images are being used for illustrative purposes only.
Certain stock imagery © Thinkstock.

This book is printed on acid-free paper.

Because of the dynamic nature of the Internet, any web addresses or links contained in this book may have changed since publication and may no longer be valid. The views expressed in this work are solely those of the author and do not necessarily reflect the views of the publisher, and the publisher hereby disclaims any responsibility for them.

Enquiries to: reverendanuli@yahoo.com

Dedication

I celebrate my father Colonel Leonard Ginikaezindu Ufodike (rtd.), for being my friend and cheerleader.

You are part of the unique puzzle
called humanity. Make the difference!

. . . Anuli Ausbeth-Ajagu

Contents

Foreword ix

Introduction xi

Chapter 1   Love Yourself 1

Chapter 2   Dream Big 8

Chapter 3   Clean Up Your Mind! 17

Chapter 4   Sacrifice 27

Chapter 5   Have Fun 34

Chapter 6   Health 39

Chapter 7   Influence 50

Chapter 8   Gender Aware 57

Chapter 9   Finding a Mentor 68

Chapter 10 The Good and the Bad Sides of Sex 75

Chapter 11 Lessons in Leadership 82

References 95

Parents are to recognize that each child deserves some respect . . . Discipline your child with dignity.

Love Sam-Amaga

Foreword

The trajectory of man as he/she navigates through the vicissitude of life's journey is strewn with unending battles. To be conceived, to be born, to live and stay alive, to set goals and succeed, to be accepted by the society and make impact, etc., is one battle after another. There is no doubt however, that the most important and daunting battle man fights is the battle for self-discovery. Many fail these seemingly simple tasks of knowing who you are and appreciating who you are, recognizing your qualities and utilizing same for your good and the good of the society. They live a dreary life and their memory forgotten soon after their demise. Those who succeed in this battle become pillars of their societies, reference points and are celebrated.

The book starts by emphasizing the need to appreciate and value oneself irrespective of others' opinion. The lesson espoused is that everyone is *"fearfully and wonderfully made by a perfect Creator."* You are not an accidental creation, so learn to be yourself and stop wishing to be someone else.

The author made it abundantly clear that youths need to purge their minds of every negative thought, shun negative influences from peers, set big goals and be prepared to make necessary sacrifices to achieve the goals. She also stressed the importance of maintaining a healthy lifestyle, finding time for recreation and above all, finding a mentor.

Cognizant of the challenges of youth, the author draws from personal experiences to highlight the dos and don'ts of attaining greatness. She has poured out her heart for youths to learn and depart from actions and attitudes limiting or inhibiting their divinely ordained manifestation.

The book is highly recommended for everyone especially the young ones, who are still floundering in the journey of self-discovery. Would you write yourself off when you have what it takes to make an impact? Remember, you are not a failure until you accept the tag.

Dr. Ausbeth N. Ajagu, *MFR, FAES*
President — Academy for Entrepreneurial Studies, Nigeria

Introduction

Life has dealt me several hard blows. I have experienced different dimensions of pain and rejection. My hopes have been raised and dashed several times like mashed potatoes. I have felt miserable, abandoned and dejected.

Growing up, I had terrible feelings of low self-esteem. I was extremely shy, timid, listless, fearful, unforgiving, bitter and suicidal. My mind was messed up and my psyche somewhat damaged. I was myopic, ignorant, gullible, and nothing short of mediocre. Today, I realize that those feelings are not peculiar. Most human beings experience lowly feelings at some point in time or the other. Sadly, many, unable to navigate through the rough tides of life, end up with chronic depression or psychosis.

Thankfully, along the line, I had a divine encounter which put me on track and my journey of personal transformation began. It has been a worthwhile journey and I have seen myself grow into a visionary, purpose-driven and confident woman. Every timid young person can too.

I am convinced that every human being has innate capacity to be a difference maker in the world. Our experiences, skills, talents and passions may differ, but nobody is on earth simply to live and die without leaving a mark. Interestingly, a very minute percentage of humanity lives purposefully. This book is not about you becoming the best global leader, but about you becoming the best you.

My heart breaks each time I see young people living like sheep without shepherd; in pathetic conditions, especially those that tow the path of self-destruction. Drugs, sex, money, fame, media, poverty, ignorance, lousiness, peers, ill-health and social environment have ruined the destinies of many. No doubt, today's pressures are more intense than yesteryears, especially with the information revolution. The internet, new media, social media and hi-tech have made life extremely fast paced. Perhaps that explains why many youngsters have a microwave mentality; wanting to get just about everything instantly! Unfortunately, many fail the character test and end up preys and victims of the present age.

Having made many mistakes myself, and shedding uncountable tears, I think I have some empathy for those going through same. That is precisely what this book is about. It is for anyone who knows someone somewhere that may be feeling second-rate, confused, disgruntled, and miserable. It is a book that will inspire you to unleash your genius, to make your life count and step into your position of influence. You may feel like a rat today, but by God, you will soon become a person of worth. The sky is large enough. You are not an idiot or moron. You have an assignment and destiny to fulfil on earth. You are part of the unique puzzle called humanity. Your contribution is imperative. The earth has space for you to fill and nobody but you can step into your shoes. Step up and shape up. Don't write yourself off.

Anuli Ausbeth-Ajagu

Chapter 1

Love Yourself

MANY YEARS AGO, like many youngsters today, I thought I was ugly. I believed my nose was too long, my skin too dark, my hair too receded on my forehead. There were times I wished I were taller and light skinned. I even fantasized about being an American, European, or half caste. Sometimes, I was not even sure of what I wanted. I was told that I had 'K' legs (knock knees), and I became overly self-conscious. Definitely, I didn't love myself! Worse still, I was also a timid, overly shy and extremely introverted child.

During my early years in school, I had no voice. I was almost invisible. I felt like a mushroom that could be trampled over easily. For many years, I struggled with morbid fear of people. To say that I was always feeling intimidated, is therefore stating the obvious. To crown those lowly feelings was my lack of vision and purpose. I simply did not like my life!

That reminds me of a man whose intellect and passion, I respect. He is Dr Ben Carson, one of the world's most renowned neurosurgeons and director of paediatric neurosurgery at Johns Hopkins Hospital. He said in one of his inspiring lectures about his childhood and issues of self-esteem, "I was a fifth-grade student, perhaps the worst fifth-grade student you've ever seen in your entire life. My idea of a good day was when I got somebody else kicked out of class. Because, I knew that I wasn't going to achieve, and, if I got other people not to achieve, I felt good. You know, misery loves company. And, my nickname was "Dummy." Years later, Ben Carson's story not only changed, but he is now a reference point globally in the field of science and neurosurgery. That surely tells us that nobody should be written off in their youth.

YOUTH AND SELF-CONSCIOUSNESS

I believe there is something about youth that makes us feel overly inadequate and self-conscious. Part of it could be the taunting, verbal and emotional abuse in our milieu. There is also the challenge of naïveté and ignorance. We probably have not taken time to groom ourselves so nobody, not even the puppy next door reckons with us. Undue self-consciousness may also be as a result of our personal inadequacies and seemingly low intelligence quotient. That shouldn't make anybody write you off. You are probably in chapter one of your life's journey; there are several chapters including the climax and denouement of your story still unfolding. You are a work in progress and it is just a matter of time before the treasure within is unveiled.

On the other hand, it could be our operational environment and popular culture that infuses us with cockroach mentality. Peers, fashion freaks, screen idols and the so-called 'happening' clique make us feel smaller than we really are. The problem could also be the people around us. Their brash, insensitive and sarcastic words pierce through our hearts like a two edged sword. They compare us with others and sow in our hearts, seeds of contempt and resentment. If not properly checked, those seeds become our Achilles heel; turning us into chronic beasts or bitches.

THE PROBLEM WITH COMPARISON

I have a younger sister. She's fair skinned, outgoing, friendly and pretty. During our growing up years, people often compared us, commending her and belittling me. That affected my psyche negatively, making me touchy and angry. I still remember vividly, the comments of two friends, or do I call them foes? They did not only make deriding comments at me, they made sure they rubbed it in very well. They went on and on comparing us and made remarks like: "you need to see Anuli's sister . . . she is wow!" I took it personal. I loathed the comparison and felt unloved and unappreciated. I didn't realize how much damage they had done, until sometime later, when I recognized that I had become irate, aloof, more withdrawn, and more timid. For a girl that was already melancholic, imagine what that did to me. My self-esteem was further battered and I crept further into my already existing shell.

THE PROCESS OF PERSONAL TRANSFORMATION

Thank God, at nineteen I found the Lord. From my early twenties I began to understand that God created me special. I suddenly realized that I was fearfully and wonderfully made by a loving Creator. That realization brought freshness into my life, and my self-image improved. I began reading and building my self-confidence. I listened to uncountable motivational and personal development tapes. I attended every seminar that was relevant to my development process. I feasted on the Bible for deliverance from evil spirits. I rejected every bad word spoken into my life and began to develop character. I practised and rehearsed behind closed doors and psyched myself up to become a better me. I fought hard to become an optimist. I began to think outside the box called average.

It is amazing how people often evaluate us by external features. No doubt, a pretty or handsome face, poise and finesse, education and exposure, certificates and credentials are all a booster to personal profiles. But hey, you are more than these! The Almighty does not create trash so never allow people conclude about you based on external features alone. Your God-given brain and character are of superior value. Anyone who thinks otherwise should back off.

Today, I am proud to be me. Without meaning to sound vainglorious, friend, believe you me, I love myself. I never wish to be anyone else; not miss world, or the queen of England nor the American first lady. I am glad that the Almighty created me in His image and likeness. I am a big plus to my world. My fingerprints are unique; my features well suited. My mission is to become the best me, and not to walk in another man's shadows.

Do You Love Yourself?

How about you, my friend? Do you love or despise yourself? Well, people may not like you, but definitely, God does, and that is what truly counts. It is understandable that you may not be miss universe or Mr macho. You may be chubby or scrawny, and may have even been labelled ugly. You may not be naturally smart or apparently talented. That doesn't make you any less human. Make no mistakes; I reiterate that God doesn't create trash. You are special. There is something about you that can never be replicated. You are an original brand.

Step Up

What you need to do is to take care of your body, inside out. It is your responsibility to nurture yourself and unveil your hidden treasure. If you don't take care of yourself, who will? Have a personal make over. Improve your sense of style; get rid of mouth and body odour. Do some exercise and keep fit. Everybody cannot have a celebrity charm, but everyone can look their best per time.

Beyond the physical, develop your mental acumen. Read widely, read specifically to give intellectual lethargy the boot. Get up and mingle. Attend a seminar, ask questions. Volunteer to serve someone you admire or an organization of value. Participate in some extracurricular activities. Listen attentively, keep your eyes open and observe. Talk with people, speak up and interact. Friend, you may be the subject of mockery now, but soon your contributions will be invaluable. Stop holding pity parties and step up. Learn to appreciate this wonder of creation, called you.

Young Leader

- Love yourself.
- Don't allow negative words get to your heart.
- Don't wish to be somebody else.
- Appreciate your uniqueness.
- Thank God for making you special.
- Loving yourself will give you the confidence you need to positively influence others.
- Personal grooming and sprucing up is evidence that you love yourself.
- Looking good and taking good care of yourself will enhance your self-esteem.
- Spoken words have power; capable of building or destroying the hearers. We must be careful

not to damage the psyche and self-esteem of others with our words.
- If you don't have anything reasonable to say to someone, shut up!
- If you don't love yourself, you can't love those you lead.

People may not love you, but God does, and that is what truly counts.

Chapter 2

Dream Big

I GREW UP IN an average family. My parents were not poor, nor rich; just average. My Dad often told me, "all I owe you is your meal ticket: secondary school education, and a university degree."

I was therefore quite content being average, in a continent where many young folks die of hunger and diseases. However, like many youths, I wanted more out of life.

During my secondary school days in Nigeria, my land of birth, my family and I watched a lot of American sitcoms like *The Cosby Show*, and *Good Times*. I was entranced by the posh and beautiful images I saw on screen. Then I began to dream. One day, I told my father that he should take us on holiday abroad. I had never been outside my country Nigeria, and I wanted to travel overseas. Daddy's response was a blunt no!

Anyhow, I kept dreaming that someday, I would go to America, Europe, and other continents of the world. I even thought that perhaps, I will meet, fall in love, and get married to an American. Perhaps that will give me the opportunity to travel to God's own country; the United States of America! That was an illusion.

Desperate Moves

After I graduated from the University of Jos with my first degree, I decided it was time I did something about going abroad. I convinced my father about the nobility of my plan, and he gave me a loan to cover the cost of a return ticket to England. However, I didn't have an international passport, and I was told that as a single lady who had never travelled overseas, it was impossible for me to get a visa to England. That information really dampened my spirits.

Along the line, my mother's relative who was a British resident, offered to help. He suggested that I got an international passport, using his surname; pretending to be his second wife, to facilitate my visa processing. He further suggested that if I got the visa, once I travelled to the United Kingdom and stayed for a while, I could file a formal divorce and revert to my maiden name. The idea tickled my fancy for a few moments, but when I thought it over, I developed cold feet. I couldn't fathom executing such plans, so I simply declined the offer and resigned myself to fate.

A Common Case Scenario

Many youths from average and poor homes understand the frustration of desiring something, and having no clue about how it would come to be. The idea of seeking greener pastures abroad has even led countless youngsters from developing countries into debasing acts. Drug trafficking across international borders has landed many erstwhile promising youths in trouble. Some end up in jail and others die prematurely in a bid to make their 'big break.' Human trafficking has become an attractive option for young ladies who end up in prostitution as a means of sustenance abroad. The question to ask oneself is, is it worth the effort? Methinks not.

Any career, business or promotion that involves you taking a fraudulent route is not worth the stress. It is a bait to rope you into something that will ultimately keep you in bondage and misery. You may be blinded by your desire initially, but in a matter of time, you will realize that when you pervert equity to gain advantage, you will eventually reap pain.

THE DANGERS OF DESPERATION

Many desperate youths, have gotten involved in drug trafficking, advance fee fraud (AKA 419), armed robbery, kidnapping, high profile prostitution, pimping, cultism, terrorist acts and other nefarious activities; all in a bid to make money, curry favours or get ahead in life. Many will lament about the un-favourable economic conditions of their country of birth, the high poverty and unemployment index, the harsh operational environment where the political *god-father syndrome* and corruption seem to be the norm, and various other inadequacies and disadvantages they have.

No doubt about it, being born in an oil rich, yet impoverished country, where majority of the citizens live below poverty level; surviving on less than USD $1 a day, isn't exciting news. It is a harsh, painful, irritating and indeed frustrating experience. The trauma of having nobody to help you; no long legs or connections in flourishing economic sectors, no political godfathers, no government welfare policies to ameliorate the suffering of the poor majority, is a severe challenge to the citizenry.

Awaken Your Conscience

I pray that the conscience of those in leadership positions, especially those in government at all levels, as well as those in leadership of flourishing business sectors; especially banking, oil and gas, telecommunications, blue-chip corporations, international organizations, donor agencies, foreign missions, spiritual bigwigs, small and medium scale enterprises; will awaken to this reality and do something urgent to address the anomaly. Many Africans are suffering, and many, especially the youths, have lost faith in their continent. The dire state of any nation, and decayed value system, should propel people to think about how to become solution providers, problem solvers, poverty eradicators, welfare supporters, development agents, humanitarian, charitable, as well as social reformers.

Don't Write Yourself Off

To the youths, disadvantaged, deprived, disenfranchised, and despairing population; realize that two wrongs can never make a right. In trying to fight poverty or injustice, when you get involved in criminality, violence, theft, bombings, bloody rituals and other illegalities, you have only succeeded in wounding the system further. No nation can flourish under perverse foundations. Indeed, only righteousness can exalt a nation because sin is a reproach to any people. So, don't write yourself off. You may have been to hell and back several times over, but God is counting on you to take the lead. Become the difference maker.

The Good News about Dreaming Big

I was talking earlier about my childhood fantasies to travel outside my continent of birth. You may be wondering if that dream came true. Well, it did! In 1995, I got married, and my husband and I wanted to go to America for our honeymoon. We applied to the United States embassy and told them that we were going on honeymoon. We were granted our visiting visas and off to America we went. Indeed, even mundane childhood dreams come true! I told you my story to encourage you to wait for the right opportunity to realize your dreams. Don't pervert the process and don't take short cuts so that you don't end up cut short. There is time for everything, and if you pursue wisdom, plan and wait patiently; someday too, your noble dreams shall become reality. Every dream is for an appointed time.

Well, that is not the end of the story. America is not heaven, neither is the United Kingdom or Asia paved with gold. I have come to realize that it is one thing to dream, and another to dream big about making a positive difference in your world. Making a difference begins in your operational environment; birthing ideas, solving problems, tackling issues and influencing people; one person at a time. For instance, this book was inspired to add value to your life and enhance your leadership drive. What about you? What is your dream?

LEADERSHIP TESTIMONIES

The Black American civil rights activist, Martin Luther King Jr., had a dream. He dreamt that one day; his children will live in a free and fair society, where they will not be judged by the colour of their skin, but by the content of their character. During his lifetime, American blacks were considered inferior; second class citizens. They experienced racial segregation. Although Martin Luther King Jr. did not live long enough to see his dream come true, his vision became an integral part of the American dream.

History was made in the United States of America on January 20th 2009, when Barack Hussein Obama was sworn in as the first African-American President of the country. Though dead, Martin Luther King Jr. must have smiled on that day. President Barack Obama was also awarded the Nobel Peace Prize the same year, on 9th October, 2009, for his extraordinary efforts to strengthen international diplomacy and cooperation between peoples. That should inspire you too, to dream big about becoming a positive change agent in your world.

What is Your Dream?

So what is your dream? Yours may be to become a great inventor. Or perhaps a scientist, communicator, renowned author, artiste, business icon, reputable politician, environmentalist, teacher, preacher, financial advisor, entrepreneur, or a good leader. Maybe you visualize your country of birth as a nation, where there is peace, progress, true democracy, good roads, uninterrupted power supply, quality education, good healthcare systems, good governance, security of lives and property, economic prosperity, sufficient food supply, minimal poverty, good welfare system, no fuel queues and good moral ethics.

You may live in Canada, America, or Europe, and find some of the aforementioned issues strange. For example, some folks have never experienced electricity outage since they were born. Welcome to the developed world! Nonetheless, every nation has its issues. Do a research on the peculiar challenges in your locality. You may observe that there is high profile crime; school shootings and killings, high suicide rate, drug abuse, sexual perversion, alcoholism, many unwed mums, psychosis, gambling, laziness, or certain iniquities in your society. Take it as your personal responsibility, to bring change. Yes, you can add value, take the lead and make positive impact in your earth space.

Indeed, dreams come true, but, make sure that your dream is worthwhile; a positive vision that will add value, bless humanity, and make you a better person. Don't get disheartened because of past failures. Don't write yourself off either. Realize that winners are simply ex losers who refused to quit. In fact, failure should serve as a motivating force for you.

YOUNG LEADER

- Start dreaming big now!
- Look beyond your family background and become an optimist
- Stop focusing on your inadequacies and limitations.
- Dream of becoming better and greater than your parents.
- Dream about how to make your village, country, continent and world a better place.

- Life is not just about you, but about your making a positive contribution.
- Don't pervert the process.
- Wait patiently for the realization of your dream.
- Leaders are big dreamers.

Dream about how to make your society, continent and world a better place.

Chapter 3

Clean Up Your Mind!

For many years as a teenager, I was tormented in my mind. I believed that most people hated me, and thought that my parents picked me up from a trash can. During my secondary school days, my father, who is a zoologist by training, bored me stiff whenever he took me through lessons during school breaks. One fateful holiday, as I was preparing for my WAEC exams or so, he was coaching me and I wasn't concentrating. It was Christmas and he angrily flung my biology textbook at me in a fit of rage. To make matters worse, I didn't like my dad because in my opinion, he was overly frugal. I must confess that I loathed him internally for being stingy.

My mother on the other hand was a tough disciplinarian. She was fearsome; very hard on me, so I concluded that she wasn't my biological mother. At age fifteen or so, she gave me a good beating for refusing to eat the moi moi she prepared with shrimps (a Nigerian steamed beans pudding). There was a day I had a heated argument with her. She was driving and I was seated beside her in the front passenger seat. Suddenly I had a suicidal thought. I wanted to jump out of the moving vehicle along the Third Mainland Bridge in Lagos Nigeria! Guess what? I would have died instantly, or maybe I would have broken my spinal cord and ended up an invalid. Certainly, my mother would have been hurt, but she would have continued with her life anyway. And who would have been the greater loser? Me of course! Well, that is the bitter truth about life, which many youngsters fail to realize. Whenever we set out on a self-destruction plan, we lose. Worse still, whenever we set out to hurt or destroy others, we become big time losers and villains.

Interestingly, my mother who I thought was my worst enemy eventually became my favourite buddy. It no longer mattered to me whether she picked me from a trashcan as I imagined (she didn't anyway). Even if one is an adopted child, there is no big deal because it doesn't make you inferior or less human. Today, my mother and I are friends for life and love each other dearly. I laugh over the past, recounting the tales to youths; encouraging them to endure childhood chastisement. Young people need to realize that discipline is part of life. The hearty counsel of a well-meaning leader may not go down well with you now, but in future, you'll be thankful for it.

Our Experiences

Folks, we all have a measure of messed up minds. Our experiences in life, exposure, backgrounds and emotional deficiencies all contribute to the way we think. The fact that you are a human being living in an imperfect world means that you will be exposed to good and evil. The preponderance of exposure invariably reflects in your attitude, values and character. Unfortunately, iniquity is pervasive. Even if your family is lovely, when you leave home, you will meet profane folks. In school, peers mock you for doing good. They make mischief and misdemeanour appear to be hip while you 'miss prim and proper' are considered razz. At this point, if you don't have the willpower, you cave in and blend.

Youths should be able to smell trouble from a distance, but they rarely do, except they learn a lesson or two about listening to the wrong voice. Realize that what you hear or watch regularly affects your mind. Your mind is like a computer; garbage in, garbage out. That is why pornography for example, is a deadly trap. So what is the way out? Keep your distance from corrupting influences. Clean up your mind, and constantly check your thoughts to delete every wicked imagination.

Yeah, you may have heard the cliché, "Cleanliness is next to godliness." However, many young folks don't care about being clean. They like to mess-up, and not clean-up. There are three aspects of cleaning up: your mind, your body and your environment. We shall concern ourselves here, with the mind.

Your Mind

Nobody knows what is going on in your mind, except you and God. The human mind is a powerful breeding ground for good or evil.

Evil Mind

An evil mind can conceive wicked thoughts: how to hurt or harm someone, how to steal, cheat or tell lies, how to commit a crime, including killing, annihilation, suicide bombing and terrorism. An evil mind is a deadly poison, capable of destroying you and others. An evil mind is immoral, selfish and destructive.

Adolf Hitler, the leader of the Nazi party, is commonly described as the world's most hated villain. He was born in 1889, and committed suicide in 1945. He evidently had an evil mind, and during his lifetime, he influenced his numerous followers negatively. Through his deadly thoughts and leadership, he authorized the mass extermination of Jews and other minorities, causing an estimated eleven million people to be murdered in the horror known as the holocaust.

The world in the last decade has become more terror prone. Human life has become cheap, no thanks to the mindless killings by suicide bombers and their cronies. These individuals and groups didn't just wake up and throw bombs. Somebody somewhere incited, brain washed or propelled them. Their minds became fertile grounds for breeding evil. What about you? What do you have on your mind?

DEALING WITH AN EVIL MIND

The way to deal with an evil mind is by cleaning it up. Get rid of your stinking thought pattern and fill your mind with good ideas. Cast down every evil imagination and reject all wicked thoughts. Like I earlier mentioned, as human beings, we all have the propensity to think negatively. We also have the capacity to incubate wicked thoughts. Little wonder, New York Times bestselling author, Joyce Meyer describes the mind as a battlefield. However, we have the choice to think positively and give up bad thoughts. You must fight to keep your mind pure.

DIVINE INTERVENTION

Dealing with an evil mind requires divine and strategic intervention. I must confess that it was the Almighty, who empowered me to clean up my messed up psyche. I prayed to God to deliver me from my warped mind-set and He did. You too can talk to God. Likewise, the Holy Bible was very instrumental to the cleaning up process of my mental faculty. Ephesians 4:23 says, "And be renewed in the spirit of your mind." That was exactly what set me free. The spirit of God! I began to see myself the way God sees me. I began to love righteousness and hate wickedness. Folks, debauchery can become alien to your life when you are divinely transformed in your thinking.

Reading and Personal Development

Furthermore, I exposed myself to good literature that encouraged and inspired me to think right. I believe strongly that reading is a powerful instrument for developing your mental faculty. Books, magazines, media columns, online articles, relevant blogs and other informative write-ups are a pool of resource that can enrich your life immensely. Several motivational seminars and resource materials (inspirational audio visual tapes) certainly added value to my mind reformation and transformation. Folks, if you don't clean up your mind, it would mess up your life.

Better Perspective

When I cleaned up my mind, I had new perspectives. With time, I began to value my mother and appreciate the fact that it was imperative for parents to discipline and correct their children promptly. Proper training and rebuke may not often go down well with the youths, but those are integral parts of parental obligation.

When Parents Err

Of course we all know that parents are human and therefore fallible. Unfortunately, there are parents who don't just make mistakes, but strategically entrench corruption in their kids; propelling them to err morally. One dear young lady who has two kids out of wedlock told me that her mother encouraged her to do so. Some parents, rather than emphasize to the youths, the importance of abstinence, encourage them to engage in illicit sex. In my part of the world, examination malpractice is encouraged by parents who bribe teachers and examiners to show their children exam papers ahead of time; a practice commonly referred to as 'expo.' This is where the discerning youth needs wisdom to dissociate from such illegalities. If you are a faithful student and prepare well for an exam, you don't need expo to make it. Respect your parents, but disregard the crooked counsel.

Despite the shortcomings and laxity of our forebears, the fact remains, most normal parents wish the best for their children. Therefore, have a listening ear. Delineate the good from the bad. Your dad might be a drunk and womanizer, but when he tells you that lazy people never amount to much, listen to him. Take his good counsel about hard work and ignore his moral laxity. Your mother might warn you to be careful about the treachery of men, yet she is a witch or serial home breaker. Take her advice and avoid being a gullible naïveté; used and dumped at will. However, avoid her depravity. Realize that honouring your parents is a divine mandate. They might not be your role model, but they still have something, no matter how little, to offer.

When Parents Teach Good Values

In trying to coach, teach or instruct the youths, there are often challenges in the communication process. Not all parents understand the art of persuasion, motivation or coaching. Thus their methodology may be outmoded or brash, but youths need to have hearts that are teachable and amenable to good counsel. Nobody ever grows healthy without stretching or feeling some pain. It is part of the process of maturity and personal development. Soon you'd become a full grown adult, functioning mainly on the foundations laid in yesteryears.

Wisdom for Today

Parents and guardians also need wisdom and better understanding to be able to effectively correct the present day youth. Times are changing, and more than ever before, the younger generation needs the love and affirmation of the adults. We must understand that discipline can be done without meanness and brutality. Spoken words can build or ruin the morale of the young ones; so be careful what you say particularly in the heat of anger. Failing to communicate effectively can cause despair and extinguish hope. Therefore, the youths and their leaders need to clean up their minds otherwise they will unwittingly perpetrate error. Friend, for your mind to become clean, you must let go of negative emotions like pain, bitterness, undue anger, hatred, malice, strife, un-forgiveness, and vengeance.

GOOD MIND

You are today where your thoughts have brought you; and your future will be the result of your regular thought pattern. A good mind is the breeding ground for phenomenal thoughts and ideas. Every good invention starts in the mind of someone. Thomas Edison, the inventor of the incandescent light bulb, was considered a genius. He patented 1093 things which he invented during his lifetime. How on earth did that happen? He made his mind a breeding ground for great ideas. He failed a thousand times, but refused to quit. He was struck with adversity, but stayed positive. As a matter of fact, the suffering, challenges and pain on the journey to greatness did not make him write off himself. Little wonder his mind worked wonders! How about you? What is on your mind?

Young Leader

- Let go of your painful past memories.
- Sweep every negative thought out of your mind and out of your life.
- Consciously and deliberately maintain a positive outlook to life.
- Expose your mind to positive and inspiring resource materials.
- Be open to discipline as this will help you deal with your excesses and put your mind in check.
- Don't use your creative mind to plot evil.
- Let love and kindness fill your heart for others.
- Avoid evil communication which corrupts the mind.
- Guard your mind and always think good thoughts.
- Whenever an evil or negative thought creeps up, reject and dethrone it.
- See yourself as a leader; leadership starts in your mind!

The way to deal with an evil mind is by cleaning it up! Get rid of your stinking thought pattern and fill your mind with good ideas.

Chapter 4

Sacrifice

So you want to be a leader? Hmm . . . can you pay the price? Are you willing to work; perspire and suffer to become a trailblazer in your chosen field? Can you delay gratification in order to build your profession or nurture a business? Are you willing to invest your time, talents and treasures for the benefit of humanity? Okay, let's say you are a student; can you start saving some of your allowance for the purpose of future investment? Can you invest your time in learning new skills of interest outside the classroom? Can you volunteer to serve others, even when nobody rewards you financially or says "thank you," or "well done?" Will you be willing to suffer and bring positive change to people who may not appreciate your efforts? Are you ready to be insulted and maligned for your noble deeds?

If you are like me, the word "sacrifice" does not particularly sound exciting to the ears. As a matter of fact, some of us loathe it because it sounds like hardship, stress, unending hard work, servitude and even death. Nobody wants to suffer, definitely not me! The reality of life however, is that sacrifice is an inevitable prerequisite for good leadership.

Anyone wishing to make genuine and enduring positive impact must be willing to sacrifice and work hard to make a difference. Selfish and lazy folks rarely make history. They only settle for what is convenient and at best become average. Leaders on the other hand, are willing to pay the price; to go the extra mile, endure deprivation, give up some pleasure and comfort, work diligently, serve, persevere, innovate, train and retrain, take risks, and ultimately die to their selfish nature in order to lead right. And they don't write themselves off or quit in the middle of the process.

THE AFRICAN EXPERIENCE

In Africa, and specifically Nigeria the land of my birth, sacrifice connotes different things. In traditional or fetish settings, the word connotes shedding of blood; human or animal. Our ancestors shed a lot of blood, including innocent human blood in the land for various purposes. Some were done in worship of a deity, some for the 'cleansing of the land' in accordance with the requirement of a deity, and some as rites of passage in honour of traditional rulers whose death rites included the burying alive of the king's servants. All such sacrifices are out of tune with the civilized world.

Poverty is known to be synonymous with our continent too. As a result, many have resorted to demeaning and inhuman means of making money. Rather than work hard to earn a living, they prefer money-making rituals which often involves the sacrifice of human life. It may sound incredulous; stranger than fiction, but it is real. Many nouveau rich folks have shed blood, including that of their loved ones (spouse, children, parent, sibling, etc.) in exchange for money!

Sadly too, many political 'leaders,' in their desperate quest for political power, shed human blood in compliance with cult requirements. More worrisome is the fact that many young folks have been involved in blood shedding rituals. Some of these are part of their initiation rites into one school cult or the other, in their quest for power, money and fame. No matter the argument of these ritual killers, their sacrifices are abominable, sacrilegious, condemnable and against fundamental human rights.

DESIRABLE AND HONOURABLE SACRIFICE

Let me state clearly, that the desirable and positive sacrifice referred to here has to do with your giving up personal comfort, pleasure or instant gratification, in order to secure the common good of an enterprise, vision or people. The New Webster's Dictionary defines sacrifice as, "to deprive oneself of something valued for the sake of another person, purpose or ideal." That is precisely what I am talking about here. Great leaders make huge sacrifices in order to turn situations around for the better.

THE SEED

Sacrifice is like a seed. You plant it and water it over a period of time. Some seeds take a few days to germinate, others weeks, months, years and even a lifetime. Don't write yourself off during your seed planting season. Things may be tough and rough, but realize that every seed goes into your future as a harvest. There are seeds that you plant that the harvest is generational. Hundred years from now, somebody will be grateful that you came to planet earth. By God, your legacy will outlive your grandchildren.

Realize also, that your seed can be planted in any soil you choose. It is your prerogative to discern your sphere of influence or opportune environment. Also realize that seeds come in diverse forms. Your idea is a seed. Service is a seed. Time is a seed. Hard work is a seed. Loyalty is a seed. Money is a seed. Love is a seed. Learning is a seed. Discipline is a seed. Kindness is a seed. Mercy is a seed. Forgiveness is a seed. Humility is a seed. Righteousness is a seed. For every good seed you have ever sown, expect a good harvest in a matter of time. Of course there are bad seeds too, and the law of reward implies that whatever a man sows, that he shall also reap, whether it is good or evil. It only makes sense to flee from bad seeds.

The Mandela Example

A classic example of a leader, who in recent history made great sacrifice for his people, is Dr. Nelson Rolihlahla Mandela. Madiba, as he is popularly called, was born on July 18, 1918 near Umtata, Transkei, South Africa. This legend was a political activist who fought for the freedom of blacks in his country, South Africa. Nelson Mandela's activism and struggle against the apartheid regime and racial segregation led to his imprisonment in November 1962. He spent 27 years in prison, before he was released on Sunday 11th February 1990 by South African president, Fredrik.Willem De Klerk.

Mandela's sacrifice paid off because it led to the dethronement and abolition of the obnoxious apartheid system. Nelson Mandela was subsequently rewarded for his years of suffering and hardship, as he became the first democratically elected state president and the first black president of South Africa on 10 May 1994. He served in that capacity until June 1999. He was also awarded the Nobel Prize for Peace in 1993, jointly with Fredrik.Willem De Klerk, the white president of South Africa who handed over the presidency to him.

One thing I like about Mandela is that he did not write himself off. Despite his pain, suffering and struggles, he kept his good vision alive, until it became reality.

Little wonder his favourite slogan is, "the struggle is my life."

Well, you don't have to be another Nelson Mandela, but you can become the best leader that God destined you to be. You may never go to jail in a quest to fulfil your vision, but I promise; you must sacrifice, and pay the price. You may not receive honorary citizenship of a foreign country, or the highest national honour of your own country in reward for your sacrifice, but definitely you shall be duly compensated. Of a certainty, you will leave indelible footprints in the hearts of those you have positively influenced. You will also enjoy inexplicable joy and a deep sense of fulfilment for making distinct contributions to humankind.

Young Leader

- Sacrifice is an important aspect of leadership.
- For you to become a leader in any business or enterprise, you must sacrifice time, effort and resources.
- Hard work is crucial, if you want to make positive impact.
- The result of your sacrifice may take several years to manifest.
- Many may criticize or persecute you for your good works, but don't write yourself off or give up quickly.

- When you have a service mentality, you will eventually be rewarded.
- When a leader sacrifices for the good of others, he or she leaves a positive legacy.

The desirable and positive sacrifice referred to here has to do with your giving up personal comfort, pleasure or instant gratification, in order to secure the common good of others.

Chapter 5

Have Fun

'HAVE FUN' SOUNDS good doesn't it? Definitely! Every young person wants to have fun. No sane person wants to live in misery. I personally hate boredom and unending drudgery. Even Helen Keller, the renowned blind and deaf achiever said, life is either a daring adventure or nothing!

However, in having fun, make certain that you know your boundaries and avoid breaking the laws of propriety, laws of God, or the laws of the land. Being young is a privilege and I believe that youth should be enjoyed, not endured. Unfortunately, many young folks have a warped and perverted idea of having fun.

To the perverse mind, fun 'means getting drunk, violence, wild parties, getting high on dope, acting crazy, reckless driving, illicit sexual indulgence, and exposure to immoral media content. That is not fun, that is self-destruction! So what is fun?

Recommended Fun

Genuine fun has to do with merriment, enthusiasm, play, amusement and social interactions that don't hurt, harm, destroy or cause social destruction. It doesn't break the law of morality either. Surely, all work and no play make life a drag, drudgery and boring routine. Imagine one reading hard materials, working tirelessly, day-in-day-out preparing for exams, working on a job, business or project endlessly. It can lead to stress, mental fatigue or burnout. Having fun adds colour and flavour to life.

As a mother, I love the excitement and enthusiasm of my children whenever we go sightseeing, or they visit theme parks, tourist attractions, nice events or interesting family and friends. Relaxing at home, riding bicycles, playing games, watching a good programme on TV, hosting family and friends, and enjoying the company of loved ones could be great fun. Even as an adult, I enjoy the thrill of going on rollercoaster rides, watching a good movie, listening to inspiring music, going sightseeing, shopping for nice stuff, going on vacation, attending an interesting seminar, or just relaxing with a good magazine or book. Having clean fun is good because it gives our lives balance, helps ease off tension, and makes hard work easier, knowing that relaxation and letting off steam are part of the reward for our labour as human beings.

TODAY'S CHALLENGE

Today's youths are bombarded with various hi-tech entertainment and media including cable TV, social media like Facebook, Twitter, YouTube, MySpace, Skype, etc. The truth about the internet is that it can be used positively or negatively. Positively, it can be used to expand the frontiers of knowledge because of the avalanche of information available. For example, you can use the internet to position your business for global relevance; marketing of your ideas, products, goods and services. The internet can equally be a good tool for research, personal development, linking up old friends and keeping in touch with family and business associates irrespective of distance. Unfortunately, the internet is also a terrible source of youth corruption. There are numerous violent and pornographic sites, as well as fraudsters who use the internet to steal, cheat, perpetrate crime and destroy innocent destinies. Don't fall prey to the evil of this information age. Don't destroy your leadership potentials by careless or indecent exposure.

Personally, I think it's silly and unbecoming for people to post lewd pictures on social media. Youths should use the media positively for good reasons; to improve themselves and keep abreast happenings in the intellectual, social, political, business, entertainment or spiritual world. Parents, guardians, teachers and leaders certainly need to guide and direct the youths aright and not allow popular media to destroy them.

Sports and Physical Activity

This is an important fact of life which youths need to enjoy and take pleasure doing. You can have fun playing football, soccer, basketball, baseball, lawn and table tennis. Furthermore, swimming, horse riding, choreography, dance, ballet, and other forms of physical activity could be not only enjoyable, but also good exercise for the body. Engaging in creative arts like drama, music, playing musical instruments, photography, amateur film making, make up artistry, costuming, painting, sculpture, and other interesting vocations could be quite exciting and positively engaging. They could even be a leeway into future career paths where you have fun and make money.

Having fun should be within moral and legal limits. If you don't find balance in your life and take time out to relax and have fun, you will burn out and eventually write yourself off.

Young Leader

- Avoid immoral or corrupt entertainment, including pornographic and unduly violent internet sites, movies or games.
- Engage yourself in sports, tourism and positive social interactions.
- Stop fraternizing with fraudsters and perverts; they are out to destroy!

- Read good literature and enjoy godly/inspirational music.
- Let off steam! Smile often, life is good; enjoy it.
- Never break the laws of God or morality, in the name of having fun.
- Restrain yourself from destructive indulgence.
- Enjoy good entertainment and relax in good company.
- Make your family members your favourite pals.
- Never toy with drugs; it isn't fun, it is self-destruction. Don't do drugs!
- Wise leaders know that balance is important for personal fulfilment.

Genuine fun has to do with merriment, enthusiasm, play, amusement and social interaction that don't hurt, harm, destroy or cause social destruction. It doesn't break the law of morality either.

Chapter 6

Health

During my growing up years, I had several health challenges. I often had nose bleeding. At other times, I had abnormal lumps on my body, particularly under my armpits. There were days I would wake up with a stiff twisted neck, and be unable to move it. I also had perennial nasal congestion; and regular runny nose. To make it worse, as a teenager, I had chronic menstrual cramps. There were days that the pain was so severe, I thought I would die. I also remember having dental problems. I had terrible toothache and several teeth extracted from my mouth.

Well, I must confess that some of those problems were self-inflicted, like the tooth decay. It all began when I got into the university, at age sixteen. I thought I had the liberty to eat all the candies in the world, which my mother did not allow me to have at home. So I went on a sweet-eating spree. Worse still, I did not brush my teeth at night before going to sleep. Eventually, bacteria started breeding in my mouth until some of my teeth rotted. I must let you know that tooth decay almost drove me insane. The pain was the worst I had ever experienced in my life; worse than labour pain!

Well, I learnt my lesson the hard way, and since then, I have taken extra precaution to maintain good oral health. I learnt to brush my mouth; teeth and tongue thoroughly, day and night. That helps to keep bacteria at bay. Friend, health is wealth! No matter how intelligent, smart, skilful, talented or hard working you are, if you are not healthy, you can never be truly happy or contented. You need good health to lead cheerfully and successfully.

DEFINING HEALTH

According to the World Health Organization, Health is "a state of complete physical, mental and social wellbeing and not merely the absence of disease or infirmity."

That means that apart from making concerted effort to avoid diseases, we should also work at having mental, emotional and social stability. Having a clean mind like we earlier discussed, is very important in this regard.

RELATIONSHIPS

Having good family and social relationships is strongly recommended. When people are young, there is the temptation to think that your family members are crap. Sometimes, in the bid to socialize, we fraternize with the wrong crowd. This is dangerous and injurious to mental health. Friend, your peace of mind, joy and sanity are fundamental to good health so avoid mingling with people whose company pollutes your mind. Profane, wild, wicked, mean, perverted and criminally minded associates will keep you tense, unduly anxious, guilty, and fearful. They will raise your blood pressure and drive you insane.

THE FAMILY AND GARBAGE

The family is the bedrock of good leadership. If your growing up years were abusive; with parents tearing each other apart emotionally or physically, the propensity is for you to become violent and mean. If you are in an environment where your father hits your mother or oppresses her, you will likely grow into a domineering and tyrannical chauvinist. If your mother was a morally loose woman, the likelihood is that you will see yourself as a sex object and participate in the debasement of womanhood. We all have a level of garbage from our past; family backgrounds, school, and environmental influence. We must consciously discontinue the cycle of evil. Fight the demons from your background and dissociate from obnoxiousness.

Similarly, if you have been exposed sufficiently to genuine love, dignity, respect, faithfulness and righteousness; you most likely will exhibit trust and integrity. You will not be an insecure leader who cheats, threatens or suspects everyone around him. Neither will you regularly misinterpret good motives, or take pleasure in hurting others and accusing them falsely. You will give people the benefit of the doubt until they prove otherwise.

Danger Signals and Drug abuse

Many youngsters out of peer pressure fall into the trap of bad company. They start taking hard drugs and it affects their health adversely. Some become violent, aggressive, moody, sick and delirious. In fact, they lose their minds! You may think there is no big deal about doing drugs; that anyone on drugs can get out of drugs easily, but believe me, doing drugs is the highway to self-destruction. Some are lucky to go through rehab successfully, but many are not. They keep going back to the addiction on and off; continue to suffer extreme mental and emotional instability, chronic depression, intense suicidal thoughts, incoherence, isolation, and premature death. Drug abuse erodes personal peace, breeds confusion, lawlessness and senseless threat to innocent lives. Taking hard drugs, or keeping the company of those who do, is deadly. Many victims never fully recover from the damage, and many don't even live to tell the story. Prevention is better than cure.

You must therefore endeavour to stay emotionally stable and mentally balanced. Family unity, bonding and affinity are important factors for social wellbeing, except in cases where there is physical abuse or sexual molestation. Like the saying goes, 'there is nowhere like home.' Parents, guardians and leaders need to guide, counsel and direct the youths aright. There should be discipline in homes, schools and sound ethical training.

The fact is that youths don't particularly enjoy good advice; they prefer to be left to behave in an unruly and reckless manner. However, only through discipline, self-control and proper grooming, can the real leader in you emerge. Youngster, enjoy your family and make them proud of you.

Health Habits

I strongly recommend you adopt good health habits, including:

1) **Personal Hygiene**
   - Bath thoroughly, minimum of twice daily; morning and night, especially if you live in the tropics, like Nigeria West Africa.
   - Use deodorant during the day to keep you fresh.
   - Brush your mouth thoroughly (teeth and tongue) minimum of twice daily. You should brush well in the mornings and brush after dinner. Also endeavour to change your tooth brush as needed to ensure it is functional.
   - Wash your hands thoroughly with soap and water especially before eating, after using the toilet, and before cooking. Also wash

your hands when you return home from an outing.
- Ladies must avoid douching. Doctors say it is a bad and unhealthy habit.
- Wear clean, fresh underwear every day, as well as clean clothes.
- Avoid sharing skin-piercing objects with others (clippers, needles, pedicure sets, etc.).
- Don't share towels, sponge or tooth brush with anyone.
- Use your restroom before leaving home to avoid or minimize the use of public restrooms.

2) **Environmental Hygiene**
   - Keep your bedroom, bathroom, house and environment clean at all times.
   - Get rid of mosquitoes, cockroaches and rats.
   - Ensure your windows are gauzed, especially in countries where parasites and rodents breed.
   - Use insecticide treated mosquito nets especially if you live in Africa, and you don't have gauzed windows.
   - Empty your trash can daily.
   - Avoid stagnant water, because mosquitoes and germs breed there.

3) **Healthy Diet**
   - Eat balanced diet rich in fibre, low cholesterol, and minimal fats.

- Make effort to eat fruits and vegetables every day. It helps in several ways and promotes good bowel movement.
- Cut down on excess sugar and salt.
- Eat moderately.
- Check your body mass index (BMI) and maintain a healthy weight. Obesity is unhealthy!
- If you eat chicken, do so mostly without the skin. Minimize the consumption of egg yolk, because the albumen is healthier.
- Minimize or avoid red meat, eat more of fish, especially high sea water fish.
- From age forty, become very health conscious especially with your diet.

4) **Exercise Daily**
- Brisk walk, dance, stretch your body.
- Jog, skip, run, jump.
- Engage in aerobics or gymnasium exercises (your doctor's advice may be necessary).
- Play football, basketball, table and lawn tennis, swim and engage in any good sport of your choice.
- Do sit ups and press ups daily.
- Physical activity—washing, ironing, cleaning, driving, and mowing the lawn are part of exercise.

- If you are obese, sickly, or have any health conditions or concerns, please seek professional advice before embarking on rigorous exercise.

5) **Water**
    - Drink lots of clean water. An average of 1.5 litres daily or eight glasses is what the experts recommend.
    - The water you drink should be pure, boiled and filtered, or factory bottled / purified water.

6) **Sleep and Rest**
    - Seven to eight hours of sleep is recommended daily, for a healthy life.

According to the National Sleep Foundation, two studies suggest that healthy adults have a basal sleep need of seven to eight hours every night.

Kristen L. Knutson PhD, Department of Health Studies, University of Chicago, further opines that "There is laboratory evidence that short sleep durations of 4-5 hours have negative physiological and neurobehavioral consequences."

The table below will give us a more detailed guide:

How Much Sleep Do You Really Need?	
Age	Sleep Needs
Newborns (0-2 months)	12-18 hours
Infants (3 to 11 months)	14 to 15 hours
Toddlers (1-3 years)	12 to 14 hours
Preschoolers (3-5 years)	11 to 13 hours
School-age children (5-10 years)	10 to 11 hours
Teens (10-17)	8.5-9.25 hours
Adults	7-9 hours

Source: National Sleep Foundation

7) **Detoxification**
   Getting rid of toxins is important, particularly as you get older.

   - Drink herbal tea
   - Seek professional advice on detoxification; i.e. recommended vitamins, fruits, etc.
   - Fast from time to time.

8) **Lifestyle**
   Your lifestyle will contribute to good or poor health.

   - Avoid smoking, and quit if you already do. It destroys the lungs.
   - Minimize or avoid alcohol—It damages the liver, especially excessive consumption.
   - Avoid premarital and extramarital sex. If you are already engaged in it, stop!

Diseases like HIV/AIDS, Hepatitis B, STDs and cervical cancer spread with sex.
- When you get married, stay faithful to your spouse.
- Avoid worrying, overworking, or negative thoughts.
- Be happy, smile and have compassion in your heart for people. A merry heart doeth good like medicine.
- Consciously forgiving, rather that harbouring bitterness, will promote good health.
- Pray daily to God for good health. My personal testimony is that God has blotted out all those childhood diseases that tormented me earlier in life.

9) **Medical check-up**
- Don't delay in seeking medical help when you are ill, or notice physical abnormalities, or have any cause for concern with your health. The fact that you are seeking medical attention doesn't mean that you don't have a positive attitude or faith. It simply shows wisdom and common sense.

Young Leader

- Live a health conscious life from your youth.
- Take good care of your body while you are young, for a healthier happier future.

- Be happy; get rid of anger and bitterness. Your state of mind promotes good health!
- Practice health habits regularly, but don't necessarily become a health freak.
- Good and godly relationships promote good health. Bad company will make health nosedive.
- If you fear God and do your best to live right, you will enjoy good health.
- When you've done your best but still have a health challenge, don't write yourself off. Maintain a positive attitude always and you'd be the better for it.

No matter how intelligent, smart, skilful, talented or hard working you are, if you are not healthy, you can never be truly happy and contented.

Chapter 7

Influence

The first and only day I ever put a cigarette in my mouth, it was a peer that gave me to smoke. I almost choked, and threw it away. It was the same peer that prodded me, until I succumbed to date a guy who she convinced me was right for me. It wasn't long before I realized I had made a big mistake, and was a fool to let her influence me negatively. Leadership is influence. The question is, what kind of influence? Positive or negative, and who is influencing who?

Who Is a Peer?

A peer is someone, who is of equal standing with another in a group.

Peer Group

According to The New Webster's Dictionary, peer group is a "group who regard themselves of equal standing in the milieu in which they exist." Peer group influence often becomes very visible in children and youths, as they go through primary, secondary school, and the university. Suddenly, you feel like belonging to the 'happening clique' of guys and girls. Members of our peer groups put pressure on us to act in certain ways, or adopt certain behavioural patterns, in order to blend with the rest of the group.

Peer Pressure

Peer pressure can simply be defined as the influence of one's friends on morals.

Bad Peers

Ben Carson, the world renowned neurosurgeon and author of inspirational books like *Gifted Hands* and *Think Big*, said, "when I got to high school, I ran into the worst thing a young person can run into. It's called peers, negative peers. P-E-E-R-S. That stands for People who Encourage Errors, Rudeness and Stupidity."

Indeed, young people often blindly follow their peers, so-called friends, to act foolishly and stupidly. The resultant effect in most cases is pain, punishment, shame and regrets.

Good Peers

This is a rare breed I consider to be
People who
Encourage
Excellence
Responsibility and
Success.

As far as I am concerned, if your peers or friends are not encouraging you to be excellent, responsible or successful in your academics, career, moral, social or spiritual life, they are not worth your time. Get wise and disconnect from the negative influences. As a matter of fact, you should be the one inspiring your peers. You should be a pacesetter, standing out positively; challenging your peers to get rid of mediocrity and become agents of positive change. Making a difference through positive influence is what makes you a great leader.

Counsel from a Wise Man

On May 27 2000, Ben Carson gave a speech at university of Detroit's 151st commencement exercise. I found his remarks very inspiring particularly the part where he asked the graduates to "THINK BIG." According to him:

The "T" is for "Talent," which God gave to everybody. Not just the ability to sing and dance and throw a ball—nothing wrong with those things . . . but, let's put intellectual ability where it belongs.

The "H" is for "Honesty." Lead a clean and honest life. You don't put skeletons in the closet that way, because if you do, they always come back to haunt you, just when you don't want to see them. And, if you always tell the truth, you don't have to try to remember what you said three months ago.

The "I" is for "Insight," which comes from listening to people who've already gone where you're trying to go.

The "N" is for "Nice." Be nice to people, because once they get over their suspicion of why you're being nice, they'll be nice to you.

The "K" is for "Knowledge," which is the thing that makes you into a more valuable person . . . "Gold, silver and rubies are nice, but we treasure far above those things, knowledge, wisdom and understanding." Why? Because with that, you get all the gold and silver and rubies you want, but more important, you come to realize that gold and silver and rubies don't mean anything, that the thing that is important is developing your God-given talents to the point where you become valuable to the people around you.

The "B" is for "Books," which is the mechanism for obtaining that knowledge, and it's never too late . . . as my mother showed. My mother did eventually teach herself how to read, she got her GED, went on to college. In 1994, she got an honorary doctorate, so she's Dr. Carson now, too. So, it's never too late.

The second "I" is for "In-Depth Learning," learning for the sake of knowledge and understanding, as opposed to superficial learning. Superficial learners cram, cram, cram before a test, sometimes do OK, and three weeks later, know nothing.

The last letter, "G," is for "God." Don't be ashamed of God. We live in a country where people say, "You're not supposed to talk about God in public . . . That's a bunch of crap. Please go forth with the knowledge that it's OK to live by godly principles of caring about your neighbour, of loving your fellow man, of developing your God-given talents to the utmost so that you become valuable to the people around you, of having values and principles and standing for something."

Young Leader

- Leaders don't 'belong' to a peer group; they 'stand-out' from the group.
- Leaders don't cave in to negative pressure; they inspire others to do the right thing.

- Leaders don't blindly follow the crowd to err or behave badly; they question the bad behaviour of others.
- Leaders have their eyes wide open and follow the path that leads to success.
- Leaders are wise, and avoid indulging in acts that are detrimental to their health, reputation, or integrity.
- Leaders don't seek cheap popularity through notoriety.
- Leaders develop good character which makes them influential.
- Leaders are well informed, not ignoramus or noise makers.
- Leaders are good followers before they become great leaders.
- Leaders are good listeners and observers, who learn from other people's mistakes.
- Leaders know that good manners; not bad manners, is what makes you really cool.
- Leaders don't repeat the same mistakes over and over again.
- Leaders don't have inferiority or superiority complex, but a healthy self-esteem.
- Leaders are trustworthy because they have a high sense of integrity.
- Leaders are readers and learners, committed to personal development.
- Leaders are ex-losers who refused to remain failures.

- Leaders are human. When they make mistakes, they don't write themselves off. They genuinely make a detour and change for the better.
- Discerning and enduring leaders fear God.
- Making a difference through positive influence is what makes you a great leader.

Are you a Leader? You can begin the process today!

Chapter 8

Gender Aware

By birth, I am an African woman, and I grew up in a society that propagates male superiority and female inferiority. I was irked by many of the injustices I saw perpetrated against my gender. I knew it just wasn't right.

Some of the issues that grieved and still grieve my heart include: male child preference at birth, particularly when the female child is treated like an underdog and some women thrown out of their matrimonial homes for bearing only female children. Other issues include violence against women (spousal battering, rape and assault), sexual exploitation (prostitution, trafficking and abuse), harassment (workplace, school and environmental), prejudice, oppressive widowhood practices/disinheritance, early and forced marriage, marital oppression, intellectual subjugation (deprivation of access to education and career discrimination) and gender poverty.

Right the Wrongs

When you observe issues that involve injustice and perversion, rather than write them off as impossible to correct, you can do something, no matter how seemingly ordinary or little, to right the wrongs. Over the years, I have personally borne the burden of contributing to correcting certain anomalies in my nation of birth and beyond. I have written books and articles geared at gender sensitivity. Some of these works include ***The King's Verdict, Nwanyibuife*** (a woman is to be reckoned with), ***Maiden, and Stigma from the Past***. I have also been published in the Association of Nigerian Authors (ANA) anthology, Women Writers of Nigeria (WRITA) / British Council anthology and numerous articles in local and international print media. That is part of my modest contribution to inspiring gender sensitivity and restoration of the dignity of womanhood. Personally, I have also championed and contributed to numerous initiatives advocating for women empowerment and gender mainstreaming. I consider my efforts as a seed into the future of women, particularly the African woman.

Leading Change

In my country Nigeria, female writers and non-governmental organizations are rising as forces against female subjugation. Even in the spiritual world, one woman who is blazing the trail despite cultural and religious prejudice is Rev. Funke Felix-Adejumo. Her voice, through various platforms, is resonating and powerful in liberating the African woman from oppression and misery. Programmes like her Mothers'

Summit, Beauty for Ashes and other impactful conferences are reaching out to women across Africa and the globe. Her books, CDs and messages are practical, topical and transformational.

In the Arab world, Queen Rania Al Abdullah, the queen consort of Jordan is using her position to advocate on behalf of a variety of causes she believed to be important. A progressive female voice in the Arab world, Queen Rania became a powerful advocate for reform in education and public health, the development of a sustainable tourism industry in Jordan, youth empowerment, and cross-cultural dialogue between the West and the Arab world. Perhaps most notably, she worked as an outspoken opponent of the traditional practice of "honor killings," the murder of women by members of their own family for perceived violations of Islamic moral code.

THE LEADERSHIP QUESTION

Are you a young female, aspiring for leadership? Don't write yourself off and conclude that it's a man's world. Sister, the world is for both male and female and we are here to complement one another. Well, culture, tradition and nature may have given men a natural edge in terms of physical strength, but nowhere was it eternally entrenched that women should be written off. It has never been proven that women are useless, worthless, or second rate in intellect and capacity.

I believe the problem is that we have simply written ourselves off! We have also swallowed a lot of cultural trash without questioning the norm. Many women are also too complacent to lift their voices against injustice. Some are simply comfortable and pretentious, shutting their eyes to gender based crimes.

Friend, irrespective of your gender, I dare you to stand up against injustice otherwise you will fall victim in the long run. Let it be known that one gender-sensitive soul tried to reverse the parochial abuse of womanhood. That person should be you, your mother, daughter, sister, cousin, friend, wife, or the girl next door. Don't write her off. Don't allow society's prejudice or negative labels to cage or stifle the woman's potentials. Give her space to influence her world positively. You can start influencing your environment right where you are.

John C Maxwell, a renowned leadership coach says, don't wait for that position, start leading right where you are. Your family is waiting for you. Your nation and continent are waiting to feel your positive impact. The whole world is your earth space and somebody somewhere needs your good vision and message. Rise up and be counted! Dear lady, don't try to be a man; don't act masculine to prove a point. Become a female leader of distinction. Don't worry about your age, start leading now! Be encouraged and inspired by the success stories of women, who despite all odds and challenges, went ahead to lead and leave indelible footprints in the sands of time.

Some Female Leadership Testimonies

- **Anne Frank** was the author of "The Diary of Anne Frank," one of the most widely read books written in the last century. She was fifteen when she died, having documented her thoughts and experiences in hiding during World War II in her diary in Amsterdam, Holland. It was Anne Frank's desire to see her diary published as a book and that dream became reality even after she had died. Hers is a testimony of courage, hard work, determination and focus, even in the midst of adversity. History still acknowledges her leading role as one who documented one of the most powerful testimonies of the cruelty and inhumanity of the Nazis. Anne Frank has proven that good dreams outlive the dreamer.

- **Sojourner Truth** was a former slave who made the journey from slave to legend because she never lost her faith in God. She was the first black woman to speak publicly, God's truth against slavery, traversing the American land, denouncing slavery and slavers, advocating freedom, women's rights, women's suffrage, and temperance.

  Sojourner was an activist at a time when she was a lone voice, but she was not deterred. One writer commented that sojourner combined in herself, the two most hated elements of humanity:

she was black and she was a woman, and all the insults that could be cast upon colour and sex were together hurled at her. Yet she became an influencer . . . a leader, acknowledged for her positive impact, strength, poise, self-confidence and faith.

- **Mother Teresa** was the epitome of compassion and love. Her testimony is proof that one does not need to be stereotype to become a change agent in society. She never got married, nor had any biological children, but she was referred to as mother, by the numerous souls she touched. Mother Teresa influenced her world through her charity works for the lepers, sick, homeless, rejected and dejected poor in the slums of India. She became a beacon of hope and leading light in a harsh and troubled world. She was recognized and rewarded with the Nobel Peace Prize for her efforts in 1979.

- **Pastor Bimbo Odukoya** was a combination of beauty, intelligence, compassion, purity and purpose. She was the renowned hostess of Singles and Married television programme, where principles of successful relationships, successful marriage and godly living were taught. She was also a highly sought—after itinerant preacher, whose core message was on righteous living. Her messages and counsel helped in the building of numerous strong families. Her books, services and sacrifices for humanity remain a source of inspiration and legacy, even after her death at age 45, in 2005.

- **Florence Nightingale** was synonymous with nursing and compassion. She was born with a silver spoon to elite parents; William and Fanny Nightingale in England. Despite being surrounded by immense wealth, the young Florence Nightingale had the zeal to help the downtrodden. At seventeen, Nightingale felt divinely inspired. "God spoke to me . . . and called me to His service," she said. She thus went ahead to study and practice nursing; caring for the sick and teaching the poor. Her greatest impact was in hospital administration. Florence upgraded and standardized the practice of nursing, entrenching hygiene and cleanliness as fundamental values in the practice of nursing. She also brought dignity and legitimacy to the nursing profession, which was erstwhile considered a disreputable occupation performed by women who were alcoholics and prostitutes. During her lifetime, Nightingale authored over 200 books and pamphlets.

- **Helen Keller** was the most famous disabled person in recent history. Despite being blind and deaf, she lived a life of outstanding achievement, proving that disability was not an excuse for mediocrity. During her lifetime, she went round the world advocating for the rights of the blind, deaf, and women. Helen Keller wrote nineteen books, was the guest of several American presidents, and became the first woman Harvard University ever recognized with an honorary degree.

Her success in life was largely due to the awakening of her potentials and personal development with the mentoring of her governess, Anne Sullivan. Keller remains a source of inspiration, teaching us that no matter the obstacles that come our way, we can surmount, overcome and become leaders through sheer determination, resilience, education, connecting with good mentors and faith.

SHATTERING THE GLASS CEILING

The world is dynamic and women are becoming more significant in various spheres of leadership. Many women have shattered the glass ceiling and risen to leadership status in business, career and politics. Several female leaders of nations are making history and leaving good legacies. The African woman is also awakening to her responsibility to her continent. In Liberia West Africa, Her Excellency, Ellen Johnson-Sirleaf became the first black woman to be democratically elected and sworn in as president of an African Country, in year 2006.

Women have also proven their intellectual and physical prowess in various endeavours; from literature to arts, science, music, environment, and peace. A Kenyan woman, Wangari Maathai won the Nobel Peace Prize in 2004 for her contribution to sustainable development, democracy and peace. She founded in the 1970s, the Green Belt Movement, an environmental non-governmental organization focused on the planting of trees, environmental conservation and women rights. Although Wangari Maathai died in 2011, her legacy lives on.

THE GENDER AWARE MALE

Men, who wish to have significant impact in our world today, must carry women along and see them as partners in progress. Fathers, husbands, brothers, colleagues, leaders and men everywhere, need to be gender sensitive and respectful of the female gender. Battering, molestation, dehumanization, and abuse of womanhood should stop. The truth about the twenty-first century is that gender awareness and sensitivity, will accelerate the progress, peace and wholesome development of nations and the world at large. It is strongly recommended that people should stop oppressing women under the guise of religion. Oppressing, tormenting, strangulating or killing women in the guise of religion is barbaric, archaic, and offensive to the true Living God.

Some gender aware males worthy of mention here include Pastor Taiwo Odukoya, who constantly seeks to empower women through various platforms like the *Woman Leader* and *Discovery for Women*. King Abdullah II bin Al-Hussein of Jordan is worthy to be commended for officially elevating his wife Rania to the Status of Queen in 1999 after he became king, and allowing her to become a voice of influence. President Bill Clinton of the United States of America encouraged his wife Hilary Rodham Clinton to maximize her potentials as New York Senator, and Secretary of State of the USA after her tenure as First Lady. Bishop Felix Adejumo has also given his wife Dr. Funke Felix-Adejumo space to fulfil her purpose. J. Lee Grady, the founder of the Mordecai Project, is also to be commended for daring to stand against gender prejudice. This father of four daughters, through various platforms empowers women and confronts abuse. Nigeria's president Goodluck Ebele Jonathan is also a gender aware male, with capacity to do more for gender mainstreaming.

Young Leader

- Recognize, respect, honour and acknowledge female leaders.
- Gender should not be a barrier to leadership because the female is capable and competent to be a partner in progress, co-developer and collaborator in the leadership of society.

- Give the female space to express her God-given positive influence in her world.
- Don't be threatened by the potentials and power of the emerging female leader.
- Recognize that God gave male and female dominion as His original mandate.
- Don't oppress, abuse or enslave women in the guise of religion.
- When you honour female leaders, you attract equal or greater honour to yourself.
- The female leader can be successful as a professional, wife and mother. All she needs is the enabling environment, determination, love and support.
- The female leader is not intimidated by men. However, she respects and acknowledges them, and is certainly not a man hater.
- The female leader is not a pervert or wacko. She is a female; proud to be a woman.
- The female leader inspires others with her vision and good character.
- The female leader is conscious of the need for integrity and ethics.
- The female leader is a big plus, not a minus to humankind.

When you honour female leaders, you attract equal or greater honour to yourself.

CHAPTER 9

Finding a Mentor

As a young girl growing up, most of the people I admired were superstars or celebrities. I guess it was the glitz and glamour of their lives as portrayed by various media that really caught my fancy. As time went by, I began to see several holes in the lives of many of those stars. Beyond wearing classy clothes, riding posh automobiles, living in mansions, gracing the covers of magazines and having millions to their credit, nothing about their lives was positively impacting mine. Many of them had serious character problems; from drug abuse, to moral decadence and reckless lifestyles. I knew that I didn't want to end up an emotional, mental, or spiritual wreck like some of them. I wanted more out of life; a noble legacy, and one that will make humanity better off.

Unconsciously, I began my search for transferable value. I began to be drawn to men and women with positive influence. I became an avid reader, listener, and personal development student. Today I realize that the more I connected with reasonable people, the more my life changed for the better. The more I accessed the wisdom, knowledge and expertise of heroes and heroines of repute, the more I desired to be a person of positive influence. I have had the privilege of learning from the wisdom of men and women of character. Some of them are leadership developers, business leaders, political leaders, spiritual leaders and heroes of our time.

Lack of Good Role Models

One of the problems our youths have today is the lack of good role models. Young people need to link up with mentors who can encourage, inspire, discipline, correct, teach, and coach them. Life has taught me that everybody needs somebody. Nobody can really exist successfully in isolation. No matter how intelligent, smart or good-looking you are, there will be times when you cannot successfully navigate through the complexities of life. Helen Keller, who had challenging physical disabilities, could not maximize her potentials until she connected with her mentor and teacher, Anne Sullivan. Youngster, you also need a mentor; a coach to guide and inspire you to your desired destination.

Who Is A Mentor?

The Advanced English Dictionary defines mentor as "a wise and trusted guide and advisor."

QUALITIES TO LOOK OUT FOR IN A MENTOR

- A mentor should be wise and experienced in a particular field of life or endeavour which interests you.
- A mentor must have good antecedents; proofs of his or her noble achievement.
- A mentor should be somebody you respect and look up to.
- A mentor must be real; not fake or phony.
- You must have access to your mentor either directly or indirectly. Direct access means seeing the person face-to-face for counsel, training or instruction. Indirect means you can access the person's wisdom through resource materials i.e. books, articles, the internet, or audio-visual materials which will offer useful direction to your life. You can also attend seminars and programmes where your mentor features. Observe, learn and be inspired!

A Dozen Basic Truths about Mentors

- A mentor must have good qualities you admire and desire. His or her knowledge must be valuable.
- A mentor's knowledge or experience may be limited to a particular field, thus you may require a crop of mentors for different aspects of need. For example, you may have a career

or business mentor, an education mentor, leadership mentor, marriage or relationship mentor, spiritual mentor, etc.
- A mentor may be hard or harsh on you or your parochial leanings.
- A mentor may not necessarily be nice and friendly to you.
- A mentor may be hard to please.
- A mentor is not your regular buddy who you can take for granted.
- A mentor may be young, middle aged or old.
- A mentor may be of a different race, tribe or creed.
- A mentor may be suspicious of your intentions, or feel threatened by your potentials.
- A mentor may have weaknesses such as arrogance, self-doubt, fear, anger, resentment, un-forgiveness, lust, ingratitude or prejudice. That should not deter you. However, you must avoid falling into your mentor's error. Learn from his or her success, but reject their character flaws.
- A mentor may have fickle emotions and mood swings. Sometimes, he or she may be very supportive of your vision. At other times, perhaps aloof and indifferent. Don't take it to heart. The mentor is human and therefore fallible.
- You are the one to pursue your mentor; to seek out his or her wisdom, and not vice versa.
- Since your mentor is human, he or she needs your validation and appreciation.

Attitudes to Avoid With Mentors

- Don't try to show off your knowledge or brag to your mentor; you might make a fool of yourself.
- Don't become a parasite, beggar or leech, or else you will be avoided like a plague.
- Always hold paper and pen when seeking for advice. Mentors are too busy to repeat the same instructions over and over again.
- Avoid over familiarity, which may breed contempt. Always respect and honour your mentor.
- Realize that your mentor is not God Almighty, thus he or she cannot meet all your needs.
- Avoid making excuses for instructions you blew. Be proactive, not reactive with your mentor.
- Avoid using and dumping a one-on-one mentor. If you must make an exit from your mentor's sphere of influence, do so respectfully.

How to Earn Your Mentor's Respect:

- ✓ Add value and contribute meaningfully to the mentor's vision, project or life.
- ✓ Give the mentor a gift, but don't steal or borrow to impress the mentor.
- ✓ Identify the mentor's need(s) and sow meaningful seeds into the mentor's life.

- ✓ Acknowledge and appreciate the mentor's contribution to your life.
- ✓ Use your words of praise to affirm the mentor, but don't flatter.
- ✓ Have a high sense of responsibility to the mentor.
- ✓ Walk with integrity with your mentor.
- ✓ Respect the mentor's time.
- ✓ If you are a person of faith, pray for your mentor.

BENEFITS OF HAVING A MENTOR

- You receive deep insights, wisdom, knowledge, education, motivation and inspiration for your life and projects.
- You accelerate your growth, since you are tapping into the mentor's reservoir of past research, knowledge and experience.
- You avoid making foolish decisions or mistakes which can wreck your life.
- You minimize tension and misery in your life because there's a trusted counsellor to show you the right path to tow.
- You draw inspiration from the mentor's travails and learn that the path to greatness is not rosy all the way.
- You grow astronomically to become a person of influence and a mentor to others.

- When you earn your mentor's respect, you may get exposure on your mentor's platform.
- The grace and finesse of your mentor rubs off on you.
- By learning from the mentor's failures, you become a better brand.

Young Leader

It's time to connect with a mentor, grow and become a mentor to others who are looking up to you.

Chapter 10

The Good and the Bad Sides of Sex

If you ask me the question, is sex good or bad? I will say both. Yes, sex is good within the confines and context of marriage. And marriage refers to a legitimate union between one man and one woman. However, outside marriage, sex is a poison, a deadly killer, subtle destroyer and waster of human destiny.

Many youths have fallen victim to the sex trap. They have been told that when you get to a certain age, you cannot do without having sex. As a matter of fact, they are told that as long as you use a condom, you are safe. They are not educated on the truth about condoms; that they are not 100% safe; that they can tear or pull out whilst in use, could be expired or wrongly used and therefore rendered ineffective. I was once told the story of a baby that was born with a condom wrapped round its little finger. Friend, get this straight into your medulla oblongata; abstinence is the key for sensible youths!

Today's Challenge

No doubt, various media, popular culture, inquisitiveness, stubbornness, corrupt environment, indecent exposure, peer pressure, fallen societal values, lack of personal principles, warped mind-sets, poor motivation, lack of genuine fear of God and lack of good role models; are some reasons why today's youths are falling victim to the sex trap. Many are getting their fingers burnt, their emotions battered, their reputation tarnished, their lives short-circuited because of sex. Folks, there is time for everything, and the right time for sex is when one is married.

Yes, Abstinence is possible

It is indeed very possible for youths to tow the path of honour and practice abstinence now. With personal determination and faith in God, abstinence from pre-marital sex is possible. When you discipline your body as a youth or single, you find it easier to exercise self-control in other areas of your life. You also discover that when you get married, fidelity to your spouse is easier since you have already learnt how to tame your body. I believe strongly that the devil, the greatest deceiver and enemy of mankind is out to corrupt, defile, disgrace and oppress the youths through sex. Don't become a slave to sex. Dare to be different, dare to lead!

Some Wrong Perceptions of Sex Outside Marriage Include:

- 'Everyone' is doing it, what's the big deal? Let me do it too.
- If I really love someone, I should have sex with the person.
- Having sex makes me feel on top of the world.
- Sex is an act of nature, which should be done anywhere, whenever you feel like it.
- Abstinence from sex is a sign of weakness.
- Virginity is like a disease and should be avoided.
- Having sex with my partner shows I am cool and trendy.
- If I don't have sex now, I will become an old hag.
- Real men have sex when they feel like it.
- The true value of a woman lies in the number of men she sleeps with.
- Having sex is a sign of growing up.
- No man will marry you except you've had sex with him.
- It is impossible to abstain from sex as a youth or single.

All the above perceptions about sex are wrong. Unfortunately, many young persons have believed and fallen victim to those lies.

The Consequences of Sex Outside Marriage Include:

- Loss of self-respect, dignity and honour.
- Cheapening of oneself before the person's partner.
- Risk of contracting sexually transmitted diseases.
- Propensity to contract incurable diseases like the dreaded HIV/AIDS.
- Higher risk of cervical cancer.
- Risk of future infertility as a result of untreated sexually transmitted diseases.
- Propensity to get pregnant or father a child outside wedlock.
- Risk of marrying the wrong person as a result of being trapped with unwelcome pregnancy.
- Open invitation to become a source of ridicule, mockery and stupid jokes.
- Guilt feelings of regret and mental trauma over a long period.
- Propensity to suspect and falsely accuse your partner.
- Propensity to be sexually abusive either as a victim or perpetrator.
- Loose moral ethics and propensity to become a sex maniac.
- Propensity to commit adultery when you get married.
- Open invitation to your future spouse committing adultery.
- Invitation of demons and demonic soul ties into one's life.

- Loss of reputation before respectable folks.
- Depletion of financial resources.
- Waste of time and energy in wrong relationships.
- Loss of talent and creative ability.
- Loss of focus and poor concentration.
- Emotional peril and heartbreak.
- Propensity to become morally bankrupt and corrupt.
- Propensity to desire and seek new sexual experience.
- Likelihood of never really being satisfied or content with your partner.
- Inexplicable feelings of filthiness and dirtiness.
- Morbid fear of the unknown.
- Shame and embarrassment especially for the female folk.
- The danger of eternal damnation.

The Way Out Of the Sex Trap

- Recognize and accept that sex outside marriage is an anomaly, it is wrong.
- Get rid of societal permissiveness that promotes illicit sex.
- Confess your misdemeanour; genuinely commit to turning a new leaf.
- Forgive yourself for your error and consciously turn a new leaf.
- Read good books and other useful resources on how to live responsibly.

- Flee from any compromising situation that would make you fall into error.
- Mentally reject and get rid of any immoral thought that creeps up.
- Avoid sleepovers at the home of someone you are attracted to or dating.
- Have boundaries in your relationships with the opposite sex.
- Deliberately exercise self-control and sexual discipline.
- Get rid of all corrupting materials in your possession such as pornographic books, magazines, films and X-rated internet sites.
- Avoid and switch your attention away from any immoral or sensual material.
- Keep away from dissolute friends because their company could affect you negatively.
- Mind your language; avoid cracking coarse and sexually suggestive jokes that could make you fall prey.
- Pour your energy into useful activities such as work, a vocation, education, personal development, practical skills acquisition, creative arts, sports or other useful entertainment.
- Never pity, tolerate, or concede to someone who uses sex as a bait for friendship or favour.
- Be self-aware and conscious of your environment to avoid being molested or abused.
- Young persons should report every sexual harassment attempt to their parents, guardian, school authorities or trusted fellow.

- Ladies, please dress responsibly and avoid wearing provocative dresses; showing off your cleavage and vital parts. This will help reduce temptations.
- If you are provoked by the revealing or sensual dressing of anyone, take your eyes off rather than glare.
- Tame your emotions and cravings. It has to do with your mind-set.
- Believe that you can control your sex urge, and you will.
- Have faith in God. Pray for the ability to tame your libido.
- Realize that when you are married, you can have all the sex in the world with your spouse.
- Also realize that there is more to life than sex so think about something different.

Outside marriage, sex is a poison, a deadly killer, subtle destroyer and waster of human destiny.

Chapter 11

Lessons in Leadership

Leadership is a serious calling. It is not a game for the faint hearted or babies. If you really want to lead effectively, you need to be well-organized. The world is in dire need of men and women of positive influence and you, my friend, are one of them. I am not just referring to people with top positions in management or politics. I am talking about people who lead at whatever vocation or enterprise they are involved in; people with a mark of distinction, who make the difference.

So if you are a student, you must strive to be better than average. You can do research, push yourself further and become a coach and role model to your peers. How about looking for areas of need in your environment, where you can make improvements and bring ideas that can better the lot of the majority? You can also use your God-given ideas, wisdom, position, power and creative talents to positively impact lives.

Leadership is Service

Leadership is all about vision and service; standing out, touching lives positively and making your earth space better than you met it. You may be young, but you are definitely not too young to make a difference. Nothing stops you from being a trail blazer either. Sincerely speaking, I believe that many old leaders have failed. Their relevance has expired. Now is the time for the youths; our generation next to take the lead. You cannot lead effectively if you are ignorant. Wisdom, knowledge and good understanding will give you the winning edge.

SOME LESSONS IN LEADERSHIP

- ✓ **Vision — Bill Clinton Caught the Vision Early:** Every leader must see the big picture of a desired future, even when everything looks distant or bleak. As a youth, you can catch a noble vision like President Bill Clinton did, when he was just a teenager in 1963. Clinton went on a visit to the White House as a representative of the American Legion Boys' Nation program; met and shook hands with the American president, John F. Kennedy, and dreamt that one day, he too will become president. That dream came true thirty years later, in 1993, when he was elected the 42nd president of the United States of America.

- ✓ **Passion** — what subjects or vocation intrigue, excite and interest you? Are you imaginative, creative, or good at selling? What infuriates or makes you mad? What brings out the compassion in you, or brings tears to your eyes? Whose burden, pain, shortcomings or issues bother you? Are you science or arts inclined? Do you talk a lot, love to argue, or love working with computers? Are you creative, imaginative and artistic? Do you love singing, dancing or acting? Are you athletic and sporty? Are you a critique? Do issues of child abuse and child trafficking make you sad? Are you a trouble shooter and peace maker? Are you angry when you observe injustice, poverty, moral decadence, poor leadership, ravaging diseases, corruption, and poor infrastructure? Perhaps you are called to be a scientist, diplomat, social reformer; an activist, teacher, human resource developer, reputable entrepreneur or political icon. What you are passionate about could be a clue to your leadership calling.

✓ **Experience — The Kemmoss Wilson Example:** From where have the bulk of your experiences and expertise come? Learn from Charles Kemmons Wilson (1913-2003), the founder of Holiday Inn, who experienced childhood poverty. His father died when he was nine months old, and his poor mother had to raise him alone. Kemmons started business at age six, selling newspapers, and hustling for sustenance. As a teenager, he borrowed USD $50 from a friend to buy a popcorn machine with which he sold popcorn at the Memphis movie theatre.

He later went into real estate and by 1950, he became a millionaire. He opened the first Holiday Inn Motel in 1952, and by 1957, he franchised the chain as Holiday Inn of America. By 1960, Holiday Inn went international. Wilson diversified into several other businesses, and died at the ripe age of 90 years.

✓ **Consistency—The Mary Kay Ash Testimony:** You cannot really become a leader in a field or enterprise where you have not been consistent in principle, service, focus, work or impact. In consistency lies your strength. Mary Kay Ash, the founder of the Mary Kay brand had spent twenty-five years building a career in the business world as an employee. She retired in 1963 and was soon inspired to start her own network marketing business, based on the experiences she had garnered professionally. Mary Kay's consistency in building a quality brand name made her one of America's most dynamic business women. She became a leading icon in the business landscape, and years after her death, the business she built remains a leading brand. You may be young now, but bear in mind that it is never too early to develop a track record of consistency in excellence. Why not start with your education or vocation, and be consistent in self-improvement and good performance?

- ✓ **Persistence—The Thomas Edison Genius:** One name that easily comes to mind is Thomas Alva Edison (1847-1931), the great genius inventor of the electrical age. He was a man with a dogged spirit, who refused to give up. His most famous invention was the long-lasting light bulb (the incandescent electric light), for which he is renowned for his numerous failed experiments and his persistence, which gave way to success. He also helped refine and develop other inventions like motion picture cameras, microphone, and the typewriter. By the end of his life, he had registered 1093 patents and had made millions from his inventions.

- ✓ **Talent Development—** Every human being created by God has a natural, innate or latent talent or potential. Not a single person came empty into the world. Some are gifted in arts, others in science, some in sports and others in special and unusual skills. You may feel that you don't possess any special talent, but if you have a teachable spirit, and you are open to learning and knowledge, your gifting will become evident. John C Maxwell, a leadership development expert says, talent is not enough. Indeed, raw talent needs refinement, training, practice, polishing and development for it to have value and be appreciated by others.

William Shakespeare (1564-1616), the renowned English poet and dramatist utilized and developed his talents for the appreciation of humankind. He began a successful career in London as an actor, writer, and part owner of a playing company. He wrote numerous plays, sonnets and several poems during his lifetime. Centuries after his death, Shakespeare's genius remains a reference point as his plays remain popular and are constantly studied, performed and reinterpreted in diverse cultural and political contexts throughout the world. Your developed talent could be the key to your becoming a leader in your field of endeavour.

- ✓ **Character**—in a world where moral values are constantly being eroded, where truth, honesty and integrity are seemingly old fashioned; words in extinction, there is need for leaders to develop character. Today's youths must be taught that no leader can build an enduring good legacy without character. Sadly, many intelligent folks at the peak of their careers are humiliated as a result of moral error. Sex scandals in high places is one of the ways by which erstwhile respected folks end up disgraced. Folks, character is everything!

- ✓ **Importance of Integrity**—integrity simply means moral soundness. It means letting your words and actions match. No doubt, many fraudsters have gained political, leadership and financial prosperity by crooked means. It is only a matter of time before their true character and dirty deals are exposed. Potential leaders must strive to live above board and consciously live a life of truth. This might make you unpopular, or you may lose material favours in the immediate and short-term, but in the long run, it is truth that will always set people free.

The Fallibility of Leaders

We must also understand that the best of leaders are human and prone to blunder. Their uniqueness however, is in the ability to own up to error; admit their mistakes, apologize, and make restitution, where possible.

A good leader must also avoid perpetrating mistakes. If you discover that you are deficient in knowledge for a particular challenge, or you feel inexplicably depressed and tired, or you are so morally weak that you lack discipline and self-control, you need to seek wisdom, direction or take a walk from that leadership position. It may be time to renew your strength, go back to the drawing board, and re-learn the rules of the game.

Sit down under a mentor and become a faithful student and follower. Perhaps you are experiencing a burn-out and need refreshing and quietude. It takes humility for a leader to seek help and indeed, humility is an important quality of good leaders. As the saying goes, pride goes before a fall, and we must constantly put our ego under check. The fear of God, good attitude and good motives for leadership quest will make the leader stand, even in the midst of storms and challenges.

The Lonely Zone—Have you ever heard the phrase, "it is lonely at the top?" Believe me, it can be. The truth about leadership is that it is a lonely zone, where only the often self-motivated can survive. So if you are a 'cry cry baby,' you may thrive better at the bottom, where you can get regular pats on the back, and plenty motivation in a tough and often selfish world. The lonely zone does not necessarily mean that you are alone or isolated from other people. It simply means that you have staying power even when others don't support you.

REAL CHALLENGES OF LEADERSHIP

ABUSE BY FOLLOWERS

The fact of life is that average folks are selfish and too self-consumed in their individual need for attention, maintenance or help. Oftentimes, the leader sacrifices over the long term for his vision, followers and recipients. Little attention is given to the leader's needs, pain, challenges and issues. Furthermore, people have high expectations of the leader. Some erroneously believe that the leader has unlimited energy, enthusiasm, time and resources to meet everybody's need. This is where leaders need divine wisdom to know where to strike a balance and not become objects of followers' or people's abuse. The leader may get angry, irritable and disappointed; and justifiably so. However, he or she still needs to exercise self-control and discretion, and avoid acting irrationally.

INSULTS AND DISRESPECT

Sometimes, the leader is deliberately insulted, disrespected, disregarded, misjudged, provoked, falsely accused, slandered, maligned, probed, taken to court and even wrongfully jailed for his vision. He or she may become the subject of gossip, envy, hatred, suspicion, intense criticism and cynicism. Welcome to the club! Sometimes you look around and feel that there is nobody who truly understands or appreciates your passion. At other times, there may be so much bothering or troubling your mind such that you are sceptical, cautious or confused as to who would have the answers to your complex and intricate cul-de-sac. I strongly recommend that you make God Almighty your senior partner and counsellor.

THE PROBLEM OF GREED

There is a risk of becoming greedy as a leader, especially when you have suffered and laboured for your vision. Many leaders become avaricious, or mismanage funds from the vision they have birthed. I believe without doubt that every leader deserves to be rewarded or compensated. Nevertheless, there must be a gauge on the leader's appetite. It is an anomaly and abuse of leadership for the leader to enjoy success exclusively. Those on your team should also be rewarded. Those to whom you have been assigned should directly or indirectly benefit from the leader's generosity.

The Conscience of the Leader

Every leader should have a conscience. You need a kind, understanding, merciful, compassionate, fair, open and large heart. Never allow pressure, prejudice, stress, bad experiences or disappointments rob you of your conscience as a leader. It is easy to become cold, cynical, suspicious, jealous, spiteful, paranoid, hardened, bitter, un-forgiving, hateful, selfish, vengeful, mean, corrupt, reprobate, and evil. You should be disciplined and firm, yet human and humane.

Sadly, many leaders have a seared conscience. There are leaders who can do anything including committing murder, just to retain their leadership positions or power. Some others are exploitative and do not mind impoverishing their followers. Friend, compassion is an imperative of good leadership. Note that a leader can become an emotional wreck and start perpetrating injustice if he doesn't pass the compassion test. As a good leader therefore, you must know where to draw the line, and also know when your time has come to allow room for emerging leaders to enter the scene.

Dealing With the Lonely Zone

Yes, it can be lonely at the top, but you are certainly not alone. Don't write yourself off. You need to love your own company. Don't just love yourself, but like yourself and enjoy the privilege of being you. Don't waste your life looking for the validation of others. No matter the challenges, be grateful and happy for the privilege of living. Furthermore, you need to network with other leaders for wisdom, direction, ideas, perspective, strategy, synergy, inspiration, motivation, comfort, counsel, fellowship, strength and comradeship.

Be open and humble, and benefit from good interaction with other discerning leaders. Young leaders need older leaders to guide them through the rough patches of leadership. Older leaders need the enthusiasm, dynamism and fresh insights of the younger generation.

Indeed, leaders need one another because challenges are not exclusive. Someone somewhere has been through the same rough road, or someone somewhere has seen someone who has been there, and can empathize with you. As you connect with other good leaders, and sincerely share experiences, God will heal, comfort, restore and make you overcome every leadership challenge. Tough times never last, but tough leaders do, so don't write yourself off.

Young Leader

- Be inspired by the testimonies of other leaders.
- Networking with other leaders will help keep you focused.

As you connect with other good leaders, and sincerely share experiences, God will heal, comfort, restore and make you overcome every leadership challenge. Tough times never last, but tough leaders do, so don't write yourself off.

REFERENCES

Ben Carson *http://www.udel.edu/PR/UpDate/00/33/carson.html*

Mandela's biography **www.anc.org.za**

National Sleep Foundation *http://www.sleepfoundation.org/article/how-sleep-works/how-much-sleep-do-we-really-need*

Pat and Ruth Williams, *How to be Like Women of Influence* USA, Health Communications, Inc. 2003.

Queen Rania Al Abdullah *http://www.biography.com/people/queen-rania-23468*

Rev. Dr.(Mrs) Love Amaga, *Secrets of Marital Bliss*, Sam Amaga Ministries International, 1996

The New Webster's Dictionary, Lexicon International Publishers Guild Group, New York, 1992.

Wikipedia, the free encyclopaedia wikipedia.org